DEDICATION

This book is dedicated to the children of the world. Never forget that you are filled with light and no-one can ever take that away from you. Close your eyes take some deep breaths and feel the peace of the light within you. it is always there to comfort and guide you!

Gratitude

I would first of all like to thank my family. For continued love, support and belief in me and my endevours. For always being there, no matter where I have lived in the world! To the little people who melt my heart constantly. I feel lucky and blessed to have you all, I am nothing without any of you!

To wonderful friends and extended family who have shown me nothing but kindness, for everything we have shared, I am proud to know & love you all.

To all of the Head Teachers and teachers in the school's I work in, for believeing in me and my intentions. For caring about children and their mental health as much as I do.

To my tribe of soul sisters and brothers, who have supported me continoulsy in many different ways. You all know who you are!
To the Maltese band 'Tribali' for their uplifting, spectacular music.

To the beautiful children who I have taught for the past 10 years. Who have brought me so much love, who have inspired me to be the best that I can be for their good. For their enthusiasm, courage & dedication. I feel lucky every time I am honoured to teach Yoga to you all. To my little Yogi's thank you.

Finally, to my absolute world my daughter Skye-Aisha, you have taught me what true love is. I have became who I am today because of your love and the challenges we have faced together. I will never stop loving you. Being proud to be your Mum and guiding you to be whoever you want to be in this world. I love you endlesley. Also to our Remmy Cat for all of the snuggles

Content

Panic Attacks
Panic attacks workbook
War Zone
War Zone workbook
I am just like you
I am just like you workbook
I can't sit still
I can't sit still workbook
Anger
Anger workbook
Money
Money workbook
Bullying
Bullying workbook
Social Media
Social media workbook
I am glad to be back
I am glad to be back workbook
Gone away
Gone away workbook
Worried
Worried workbook
Sun Fairy
Sun Fairy workbook
I have two homes
I have two homes workbook

Left out

Left out workbook

Shy

Shy workbook

Hearing

Hearing workbook

Dry Patches

Dry patches workbook

What I look like

What I look like workbook

Peer Pressure

Peer Pressure workbook

Phones

Phones workbook

Pre-teen

Pre-teen workbook

New school

New school workbook

Name Calling

Name calling workbook

Adopted

Adopted workbook

Grief

Grief workbook

One parent

One parent workbook

Arguing

Arguing workbook

Be Kind

Be kind workbook

Karma

Karma workbook

Please do not wind me up

Please do not wind me up workbook

Mother Nature

Mother Nature workbook

Different country

Different country workbook

Everyone is good at something

Everyone is good at something workbook.

Note from the author.

I hope you enjoy my book of poems about children's experiences and feelings
I have been greatly inspired working as a Children's Yoga and Meditation teacher
in School's for the past ten years and offering nurture groups to children who
need a little bit of support, in lots of different ways.

As we all know, sometimes children find it really difficult to express themselves
and to speak up. It can be difficult to understand what a child is feeling or
experiencing in their lives. Especially when it comes to life changing events.
I have found that children want to please adults and sometimes carry a lot of weight
in their emotions, by putting on a happy face. Or else expressing negative pent up
emotions in a unproductive manner.
I am hoping that this little book will help children to understand themselves and others.
Help them to express and open up to their feelings by filling in the workbooks on each
poem and helping to discover their true feelings in a healthy enviroment. This book can
assist healing in adults who have unresolved feelings and emotions. By bringing
awareness to childhood experiences that may have been taken for granted.
Not realising at the time how impactful they have been to their life, personalities and
decisions. Sometimes positively or negatively.
Hopefully bringing some freedom and light through the awareness.

I am hoping through my words, that the world will become a more compassionate,
empathetic and accepting place. Allowing each person to be themselves and
proud of who they are.
I have experienced first hand the challenges that children can be faced with in life.
My wish is to bring awareness, to help the nurturing and understanding of our
children, to increase self-esteem, confidence, acceptance. A belief that anything is
possible, and most of all that everyone is loved and deserves joy and inner peace
regardless of the circumstances they may be faced with.
Lots of Love, light and positive vibrations to you all. Xxx

PANIC ATTACKS

I don't know why I get so scared;
I can't breathe and become so shaky.
My heartbeat thumps hard in my chest;
I feel like it is going crazy.

I cannot say why it is happening
Or what it is that sets me off,
Something is making me feel afraid
I don't know how to get it to stop.

Maybe it is the thought of a test;
Or a subject I do not like;
Could be that my friend is ignoring me,
Or someone wants to fight.

I find it hard to catch my breath;
I am breathing from my chest.
My mind is blank, in a trance,
I don't know what to do for the best.

Once the panic is over
I can take a full deep breath again,
I always feel so tired and low
The worry hurts my poor brain.

Ctd…

Thank you for those who stay with me
Who guide me through the storm,
Soon I will be back to me again
I can carry on as norm.

I am trying to learn some new techniques
To help me when the panic sets in.
It completely takes over me,
I would love to catch it before it begins.

I hope that when I get older
I will panic less and less,
I want to live a happy life,
Not one that is full of stress.

Panic attack workbook

Is there a time when you have felt anxious? When, what happened?
School, i am bullied multiple times i have been threatened to be jumped in school and out of school, being scared to leave the house and comments everyday that are still on going.

How did it make you feel?
scared, unwanted, useless, odd one out, imposter, worried, sickened, always being targetted.

What helped you to feel better?
nothing really.

List three things you could do to help yourself or someone else when you feel a panic attack starting.

1) breathing techniques
2) go to trusted person
3) be alone and calm myself down

WAR ZONE

I was woken with a mighty bang
I could hear screams from my brother;
I realised that a bomb went off
I had to run for cover.

Smashing windows, drumming bullets,
Their shells sounding like tin cans,
I cannot find my family,
My head is in my hands.

My body will not stop shaking,
The tears are running down my face
I wish I had my teddy bear,
To keep me nice and safe.

My street has now disappeared
It is just rubble on the floor,
Where on earth are my family
Will I not see them anymore?

The bombs keep falling through the night,
So much devastation,
Screaming voices everywhere
There is a lot of aggravation.

Ctd…

The rest in nothing but a blare;
I am cold and numb inside.
I don't know where my mummy is;
I think she must have died.

There are lots of children just like me,
Lost, hungry and afraid,
Feeling like we are in a dream,
Waiting for the noise to fade.

Some strangers have come to rescue me,
Flown me to another country,
Trying to find me somewhere to live
Maybe with a new family

I cannot understand why this has happened,
My heart is as cold as ice
I just want to be home with my family,
But thank you for being so nice!

War Zone workbook

How do you think they feel having to leave their family/country behind?
sad, worried, confused

Name three things you love about your family.
1) caring

2) there for me

3) loving

Name three things, you love about your country.
1) calm

2) nature

3)

I AM JUST LIKE YOU

I may be a little bit different;
My words do not always come out right,
But I notice everything around me,
I think I have a good insight.

I notice when you are staring at me
When I am clapping or jumping around,
When I am singing at the top of my lungs,
Then told to sit back down.

No-one really plays with me
They think I am strange and weird.
You should see me on the trampoline,
I am a jumping and bouncing wizard.

I am a brillaint runner
So very quick and fast,
You should see my Dad
Trying to keep up,
He never stands a chance,

I am actually quite funny you know,
I love to make people laugh,
I am very good at painting,
I love to splash when I am in the bath.

Ctd…

Horses are my favourite animal,
I like the colours orange and blue,
I love holidays with my family
Visiting animals at the zoo.

If you would just take a minute,
To give me the time of day,
You will see I am really just like you
But in a different little way.

I am just like you workbook

What is your favourite animal?

monkey, dog, rabbit, hamster

What is your favourite colour?

yellow

Where do you like to go?

anywhere and nowhere

Who are your friends at school?

their all fake

Why do you like them?

i don't, my only bff lives in another country

I CAN'T SIT STILL

I am always told to be quiet,
To stay still and not to move off my chair;
To stop fiddling, touching and talking,
Even to stop twiddling my hair.

I know I have a problem,
Everyone else knows it to,
My thoughts are over-active
My nervous system is through the roof.

I try so hard to listen.
I really want to know,
But so many things distract me,
My mind is always on the go.

I can hear the sounds of the birds outside,
The voices near the door,
The click clicking of a pen top;
The tapping of shoes upon the floor.

So many sounds around me,
How am I supposed to concentrate and listen,
The teacher wants me to understand everything
I really want it to be my mission.

Ctd…

Then I remember Yoga breaths;
Slowly breathe in and fill my tummy,
I follow the breath coming in and out of my nose,
At first it feels a little bit funny.

But as the time is passing,
I slowly begin to find;
That with these breathing exercises
I can quieten down my mind.

Even if it's just a few minutes
That I am able to break the spell,
At least I know I have tried my best
Please remember I have as well.

I can't sit still workbook

Do you sometimes find it difficult to sit still and concentrate?

yes, very often, school, home, anywhere

Is there anything that helps you?

nope nothing

Try this little exercise: take a long slow deep breath through your nose and fill up your tummy like it is a balloon, then breathe out even slower, through your nose letting all of the air come out of your tummy. Do you feel calmer?

If you keep on doing this you will feel calm and find it easier to concentrate. If you feel like it did not work for you then do it for longer until you feel the shift in your body and mind. You should notice that you feel a lot more relaxed and peaceful.

Try it now see if you can do this breathing exercise 10 times then write down what you notice about how you feel.

ANGER

Sometimes I feel so angry
Like my head is going to explode,
My fists all clenched, my chest so tight,
I go into robot mode.

It does not matter who is around me,
I may blame you for how I feel,
You may get the brunt of my anger
If I lash out and you are near.

Once I feel calm and back to me,
I feel upset and sad,
I do not like feeling angry or
Becoming so terribly mad.

I've learned at school its ok
To sometimes feel annoyed and angry,
But I have to control how I react
So I don't become too nasty.

When I feel the anger rising inside me;
I can notice and not let it worsen.
Remove myself from where I am
So I do not hurt another person

Ctd…

I can take a minute for myself
Count from one to ten,
I can take deep breaths in and out
To re-set my brain again.

I can think of 5 things around me
That I can see right away,
I can think of 4 thinks I like to eat and drink
To keep my anger at bay,

I can think of three things that I like to touch
Like my cat, my hair or squishing a bean,
I think of two things I can hear right now,
Like a car or a song from Queen.

I can think of one thing that I like the smell of:
Like the swimming baths or my nannas house.
Check inside see how I feel,
Now I am as quiet and calm as a mouse.

Now back to my breathing,
I take my breath all the way in and out of my belly,
My lungs filled With so much oxygen,
Angry now?
Not on your Nelly.

By the time I have used all my senses,
I will not be angry anymore,
I can sit reflect and see what triggered me,
It doesn't have to be a chore.

Ctd…

Each time I remember to do this,
My anger will become less and less
I can really see an Improvement,
Will I do it again?
Definitely yes!

Anger workbook

Can you see five different things around you right now? Name them below

1. bag

2. wardrobe

3. phone

4. Desk

5. bed

Can you think of four things you like the taste of?

1. Donnameat

2. ice-cream

3. pasta

4. chocolate

What three things do you like the sound of?

1. music

2. music

3. music

Are there 2 things you love the feel of?

1. pets

2.

Think of one thing you like the smell of?

1. perfume

MONEY

Some kids families have loads of money,
Have all the latest gadgets & fashion,
The newest phone, Xbox & Nintendo
Could you really quite imagine.

My family doesn't have much money,
Hand me downs from my brother is what I wear,
Even though my parents work very hard,
We do not have any money to spare.

Yet my Mum says we are rich in our hearts
Cos we have lots of love between us,
We play board games, twister and have trips to the park
Sometimes a picnic is a bonus.

We love watching films together
Cuddling up on the sofa,
Sharing popcorn, snacks and sweeties,
My brother always takes more cos he is older.

You may have more money than us,
It does not make you a better person,
Maybe you have all the luxuries,
But there is always a humble lesson!

Ctd…

See one day when I am older,

I am going to make this world fare,

That everyone who works so hard

Will all have an equal monetary share.

Money workbook

Name three things that you like to do together as a family.

1) board games, roblox

2) outside, shopping

3) spend time together in general

Do you have some favourite films that you have watched all together? What are they?

home alone at christmas and then just Disney films and turner and hooch.

List three things that you think make someone a nice person.

1) there for eachother
2) doesn't judge
3) nice heart / caring

BULLYING

Why are you so mean to me
Look at me with such hatred?
I always try to be nice and smile,
But you just pull horrible faces.

You push when you walk past me,
Try to trip me up or make me drop my books,
Have kicked my leg,
Shoved me to the ground
Always give me horrible looks.

You and your mates think it is funny,
That I am your punching bag,
Using me as an outlet,
For all the self-hatred you have.

It seems to make you happy
When you are hurting someone else,
I wonder if the same is happening to you,
Why don't you ask for help?

I really do feel sorry for you,
Being such a big bully is an awful shame,
Deep down it means you are the weak one,
Bullying is just so lame.

Ctd…

I hope one day you will feel sorry,
For the fear you are creating,
Get all the help you need,
So you just stop all the hating.

Because when you are a bully
One day someone will do it to you,
Then you will know just how it feels
There will be nothing you can do.

I think it is better to have real fun
Instead of being so horrid to others,
Find out what makes you feel good inside
Develop some new hobbies

It is never too late to grow up,
Or to even change your ways,
Become a nicer person
In so many different ways.

You will feel so happy and calm inside,
Have fun with many new friends,
You will not get into trouble, shouted at,
Or ever be called a bully again.

Bullying workbook

Is there a time that you have been bullied? What happened?

yes i have been severly bullied by too many people i have been told to unalive myself and been threatened that when i leave my house or any where i just get battered

How did it make you feel?

wanted to die, sick, weak, target, useless, depressed, self conscious, unwanted, hated for who i am as a person.

What happened for you to feel better?

nothing.

Because you know what it feels like, would this stop you from bullying someone else? If someone made you upset or angry, what would you do instead?

i would never bully anyone, nobody deserves it. i would try and stick up for myself. my anger would just burst out.

29

SOCIAL MEDIA

I saw a photo of you today,
That you had posted on a social,
Your hair so perfect, your makeup too,
It soon became a global.

I looked in the mirror at myself,
Wondering how I can look like you do?
All the attention, love and nice messages,
How I wish that I was you!

Your clothes look so amazing and cool,
How do you stay so thin,
I try to eat very healthy,
I even tried lifting weights at the gym.

But no matter what I try and do,
I am just not very popular;
I do not have you looks, your hair,
My skin is not that nice colour.

Hold on a minute what I have just seen
That your picture is infact edited,
The original photo that I can see
Looks nothing like the one so credited.

Ctd…

I realise that not every image I see
Is real most of the time,
The technology can change your face and body shape,
Even the colour of your eyes.

It is better just to be yourself
As natural as can be,
Real beauty does come from inside you,
It is not always what you see.

When you are scrolling through the socials,
Please remember just like me,
That most things are not what they seem,
Not what or who they appear to be!

Social Media workbook

Do you ever wish that you looked like someone on social media? If so, why?

yes, i just hate myself.

Can you tell the difference between a natural image and a digitally enhanced one?

yes, but still wish i looked like the picture.

Name three things what you love about yourself?

1)

2)

3)

Why do you think it is important to love yourself as you are?

to try and accept that you, are you not anybody else

I AM GLAD TO BE BACK

You haven't seen me for a while,
I have been very sick,
I have spent a lot of time in hospital,
My body feels very stiff!

I have laid down in bed for weeks and months,
I have hardly been able to move.
I was weak and tired most of the time
I could hardly eat my food.

I used to lie and daydream
I was at school playing with all my mates;
Running around the playground,
Slamming the football into the gates.

I cannot tell you how much I have missed school,
There is so much I need to learn,
I've missed all the lessons;
Playing games and even taking my turn.

The hospital was a long way from home
My parents always looked sad,
But now I am getting better
I feel so very glad.

Ctd…

I am getting stronger every day
With your help I will be,
In no matter of time at all;
Back to being me.

So, if I look a little tired and
I am not always right on track,
Just know that I am in recovery
I am just so glad to be back.

I am glad to be back worksheet

Do you know of a person who has been very poorly? Who?

How did it make you feel?

Is there anything that you can do, to help them or someone you know who is in hospital now, to feel better? What would you do?

What would you do to be kind once they have returned home or back to school to be nice?

GONE AWAY

My Daddy has gone away today,
I do not know how long for,
I am scared he will forget about me,
Will I not see him anymore?

My family said that he has a new job,
Somewhere far away,
We will not be able to contact him
Or even go to stay.

I feel so sad and heartbroken,
That I will not see him for such a long time,
Mum says that we have no choice,
I will miss my daddy, being mine.

Will he be able to call me,
To see how I am doing?
I want to tell him all my news,
This is just so confusing!

What if someone is horrible to me
Who will give me the advice?
Who will play basketball with me,
Or roll around having toy fights?

Ctd...

I know my Daddy loves me,
Because he has told me this before,
But I feel so frightened and disappointed
That I will not see him anymore.

I feel such a sadness inside me;
I don't know how to get it to leave,
I'm told to be strong and carry on-
But I don't know how this can be.

My Daddy has always been my strength;
Helps me with anything,
So how am I supposed to live without him now?
The thought is such a scary thing.

I am told time will make it easier
That I will learn to carry on regardless,
I will wake up every day and give thanks
Try to be positive and let go of the sadness

At least I have the memories
To think of if I feel too sad,
I can think of my daddy all the time
Remember the good times that we had.

Gone Away workbook

Is there anyone who you do not see any more who you miss? Who?

Can you think of three things about them that you admire? What are they?

1)

2)

3)

If you could say something to them, what would it be?

WORRIED

I cannot stop worrying
My Nanna is very sick,
She has been taken to hospital,
My Auntie said she is feeding with a drip.

My Granda looks so very sad,
He is missing her so much,
I wish there is something I could do,
We all love her so much.

Me and my Nanna get on so well,
She is always there for me,
She gives me lots of cuddles and sweets,
Sometimes she lets me sleep.

My Nanna is very kind to me,
She gives me loads of gifts,
If my Mum is working and I finish school,
My Nanna gives me a lift.

Nanna takes me to go shopping,
She likes to talk a lot,
She has so many friends all around,
We always have to stop.

Ctd…

Whenever I feel sad or down,
My Nanna is there for me,
Always someone to talk to
Who wants the best for me.

I pray that my Nanna feels better soon and
Is home where she belongs,
So we can dance around the kitchen
Singing our favourite songs.

Worried worksheet

Name three things you love about your Nanna/Grandad or favourite relative?

1)

2)

3)

Can you think of three or more of your favourite childhood memories and list them here?

1)

2)

3)

SUN FAIRY

Some things they make me worry
Because there is nothing I can do,
The ill-treated animals, violence,
Viruses and disease too.

My sister sometimes worries
She says she has no money,
We do not have a car in our house;
We are always leaving in a hurry.

So many people are starving hungry
Living in the streets,
Even people who faught for our country,
Have no where warm to sleep.

Some people loose their jobs,
They cannot find another one;
They are told they are too old to start again;
That nothing can be done.

I want to be a sun fairy,
Send light to all the world,
To everyone who needs it,
Every man, woman, animal, boy and girl.

Ctd…

I ask the sun to give me extra light
So I feel it in my heart,
I stretch my arms around the world
Then let the light depart.

It touches every single living being,
Brings them some hope, joy and a smile,
Sending positive light and energy
Up down all-around, mile for mile.

If something is worrying you today
You feel sad and do not know what to do,
Ask the sun for Some healing light
Then send it out from you.

Sun fairy workbook

Name three things that you want to send some light to today.

1)

2)

3)

Think of three people you could send light to right now.

1)

2)

3)

If you close your eyes for a second and imagine that the sun is filling you with healing loving light. Spreading to every cell in your body to all of your organs, from your head down to your toes. Then the light expands all around you, like an invisible bubble of sun. Know that you are always filled with light. No-one can ever take it away from you. Whenever you follow your breath into your body you connect with your inner light and peace.

I HAVE TWO HOUSES

My Mum and Dad are no longer together,
My house is not the same.
Now I have two families,
My Mum has changed her last name.

I live between two houses
It all feels a bit strange,
I never know if I am here or there
It feels like it is a game.

My Dad has a new girlfriend
My Mum has a boyfriend too,
Two strangers I don't really know,
All living under my two roofs.

I have new brothers and sisters,
I have to share my parents with them,
I only hope they will be nice to me,
I will try to be nice as well.

Even though it all feels strange right now
I am sure things will work out fine,
If we are all happy, try our best
Hopefully get along well in good time.

Ctd…

I love my Mum and Dad so much
I still need lots of cuddles,
I hope we still play as we did before and
They don't forget my bedtime snuggles.

Now I have two of everything,
My new bedroom has lights which are fluorescent,
There is one thing I cannot wait for though,
My birthday when I have two lots of presents!

I have to houses workbook

Do you have one or two houses?

Who lives in your house/houses with you?

What is your favourite thing in your house?

List three things that you feel grateful for in your life.

1)

2)

3)

LEFT OUT

Today I feel so very sad,
My friends all left me out,
I was walking around on my own,
No-one shouted me out.

I spent playtime all alone
Watching them laugh
Having such fun,
Why is no body noticing me,
Whatever have I done?

My teacher said
I know how you feel child,
This happens to everyone;
It is ok to have these feelings but,
There is something that has to be done.

You must learn how to feel happy
Even when you are on your own,
Because this is how we become stronger,
How we learn and how we grow.

Make fun for yourself little one
This sad feeling will disappear,
You can choose to feel happy again
Once you have shed a tear.

                                                                  Ctd…

Maybe you can look around the playground
See if there is someone alone like you,
Maybe you can ask them if they are ok
If they need someone to talk to.

There is nothing like your own company,
To be alone with your thoughts,
You can imagine something wonderful,
Like you are riding around on a horse.

Maybe you can sit in silence
Looking up at the sky,
See if you notice any patterns
Or any birds flying up high.

You could imagine you are in a magic bubble
It will take you anywhere you please,
Maybe you could whizz off to Italy;
To try some wonderful cheese

The next time it happens,
That you get left alone
Take the opportunity
To be happy on your own.

Go into your own magical world
It really isn't that bad,
You may make it happen more often yourself,
Being alone will make you feel glad.

Left out workbook

Is there a time you have felt left out? What happened?

yes, daily, all the time

How did it make you feel?

unwanted, useless, hated, not normal.

What did you do?

was sitting alone by myself, i needed time alone.

What will you do if you feel like that again?

accept it, ignore it and isolate myself from everyone. over think everything and try to calm myself down.

SHY

I like to keep myself quiet,
I am afraid of saying the wrong thing.
I get embarrassed very easily,
Especially if I am made to sing.

My emotions take over me all the time,
There is nothing I can do,
You may be loud and noisy;
I am just not the same as you.

I am ok with being quiet and shy,
I need time to feel myself,
Slowly I will open up,
You will think I am someone else.

So please do not ask me questions
Or put me on the spot,
You see when you are shy and scared,
It is hard to say a lot.

So please be patient with me,
I will speak up when I feel it is right,
Sometimes I really want to speak out
But I get too much of a fright.

Ctd…

Just because I am more timid
Doesn't mean I am boring or thicker,
I have lots of hobbies and interests
I love painting Warhammer figures

I do have quite a lot to say,
My own opinions too,
I'd just rather keep them locked inside,
Until I know your friendship is true.

Shy workbook

Is there a time when you have felt shy? When?

Do you feel comfortable speaking up?

Do you know anyone who is shy? Who?

Name three things you could do to help yourself or another if you felt shy.

1)

2)

3)

HEARING

I cannot hear a sound you know,
Can you imagine how it feels?
To not hear the birds chirping away,
Or the clip clopping of someone's heels.

If you call my name and I do not answer,
I am not ignoring you at all,
It is just that I have to read your lips,
You must look at me so I will know.

It can be really annoying and lonely,
Not knowing what is going on,
By the time I catch up to my friends,
They have already moved on.

I cannot hear music playing
Or the sound of a guitar,
I cannot join in with my family singing,
When we are all out in our car.

I am very good at reading lips
To work out what people are saying,
Facial expressions say it all,
Especially when we are playing.

Ctd…

I can tell if someone is crying or sad
Without even hearing a word,
I can offer a hug or a great big smile
To show that I am concerned.

Concentrating is my superpower
I think I do it well,
For if I look away for a second then,
I will not know what you have said.

Now I am learning sign language,
So I can speak and hear with my hands,
This is just so amazing communicating,
Without a word or hearing a sound.

Everyone should learn to sign,
It is such an amazing skill,
Then deaf people can always feel included;
That would be absolutely brill!

Hearing workbook

Name three things that you like the sound of?

1)

2)

3)

What do you think it would feel like if you could not hear anything at all?

Do you think that everyone should learn sign language at school? Why?

What is your superpower?

DRY PATCHES

I am covered in dry patches,
Little bits from my head to my toes.
No need to flinch if I brush past you,
Cos everybody knows.

Dry skin is not contagious,
You cannot catch anything from me,
Even if I scratch my flaky skin,
It does not mean that I have fleas.

It is something I have to live with,
Clear skin is my dream,
It is such hard work and makes me tired,
Applying all of the cream.

Not one of us are perfect,
My skin does not change who I am,
I still feel so lucky to be alive,
Some people have no arms or hands.

Remember to keep your comments to yourself
They really can be quite mean,
Looking at me like I am dirty,
When I am actually very clean.

Ctd…

Dry skin is no big deal to me,

It can happen to anyone,

Treat others how you want to be treated,

In-case one day you are one of them.

Dry patches workbook

Have you had itchy skin before? If so how come?

Name three things you think a person would feel, who has dry patches that everyone can see.

1)

2)

3)

Do you or someone in your family have a condition that you have to treat? Like Asthma and use an inhaler.
Name them below.

WHAT WE LOOK LIKE

Why do people think it is ok
To say that I am too thin,
I am just a child who is growing
Trying to fit in.

My friend gets called names for being too big,
They say she stuffs her face with food,
They don't care that it isn't true,
Or for being so nasty and rude.

A boy gets called horrible names
Because his hair is bright ginger.
Another gets bullied all the time because
His parents are from Asia.

We are all so very different,
No-one is the same,
Some people's skins are very dark
Some are very pale.

Some people wear glasses,
Or have no hair at all,
Some people need a wheelchair,
Others really tall or small.

Ctd…

We cannot help where we are from
Or what we look like too,
What would you say if all the nasty words;
Were aimed right back at you?

We all have a right to be loved as we are,
I am a nice person and very kind,
No matter what we look like on the outside,
What matters most is what's inside.

What we look like workbook

What colour is your hair?

What colour are your eyes?

Name three or more good qualities that you have as a person.

PEER PRESSURE

Peer pressure can be healthy,
Like when playing as part of a team,
Encouraging you do be strong and brave,
Like scoring a goal or fulfilling a dream.

To push you to trust yourself enough,
To audition for a part,
To apply to be on the swimming team,
Or to finish that piece of art.

A peer could be someone you admire from afar,
Who you have never even met,
Someone who you strive to be as good as,
Could be a film star, singer or a vet.

It is great to have good peers,
Having friends who you can talk to,
Who experience the same things in life,
To know what you are going through.

Sometimes the pressure will not be good,
It can be scary or exciting,
Trying to get you to do something,
You do not want to do
Make you feel a little frightened.

Ctd…

Saying "Come on now, have a go –
Everyone else is doing it",
"Help yourself don't be shy,
If you don't you will look like an idiot".

These are the times you must be brave and strong
Stay true to who you are,
Knowing what is right and wrong,
Just push them away so very far.

For if people try to persuade you,
Or you have to do it to look cool,
Know then that these are not your real friends,
They are the ones who are being the fools.

Just get away as quick as you can,
Call someone you can trust,
Getting away from the situation
Is definitely a must.

That's where real strength lies,
Being able to say no,
Say bye I have to go now,
Someone is here to take me home.

Best friends will never pressure you,
To do anything that is not right,
Infact they will do the opposite
Never try to fight.

Ctd…

Don't be afraid to let go of people,
There will always be others to hang out,
Even though they seem to be helping you,
by providing what is not right.

Your life is very precious,
Caring for yourself is the best decision,
Choosing friends wisely
Will put you in the best position.

Life is a crossroads,
Good or bad the choice is up to you,
To want the best for yourself
Or the worst,
You can choose this too!

Peer Pressure workbook.

Has anyone ever tried to make you do something that you did not want to do? What happened?

How did that make you feel?

Do you ever feel pressured to do something/say something that you do not want to, just to keep your friends?

Give an example?

Will you practice saying no to friends when you don't want to do something?

What would you do instead?

PHONES

I try to get your attention,
I say your name a hundred times,
Then you tell me to be quiet,
When I am sad you call me a twine.

You see I have big competition,
There is something that you love much more than me,
I just want to tell you about my day,
There are loads that I have achieved.

I managed to get all of my maths right,
That is a first; yippee
I've been chosen for a part in the play,
Do you want to know who I will be?

At lunch time I was crying,
I fell and banged my head;
I ate all of my lunch up again,
I had soup and some buttered bread.

I know you may be busy;
You have other things to do instead,
But I really want you to play with me,
Until it's time for my bed.

Ctd…

I want you to read me a story
And again please repeat,
To make me laugh,
Let me talk,
Lie with me until I sleep.

I've learned to entertain myself,
But sometimes it makes me sad,
I can do things for your attention,
Even if they make you mad.

Finally, you are looking and talking to me,
Even if you are so angry and loud.
I wish phones did not exist,
I just want to make you laugh and feel proud.

I suppose I must wait for the day,
That I have my own phone too,
So I can stare at it,
Ignore everyone around,
Be in my own world just like you!

Phones workbook

How does it make you feel when you are being ignored?

What is your favourite game to play?

What are your favourite stories to hear or read?

Do you think there should be rules around phone use? If so name three.

1)

2)

3)

PRE-TEEN

I know I am becoming moody,
I roll my eyes all the time,
Some people irritate me,
Even when they are being kind.

I seem to be angry for nothing,
I loose my temper very quickly,
I do not like the taste of my favourite foods,
Some of them make me feel sickly.

I cannot stand being told what to do,
Cleaning my room is just so boring,
Everyone seems to be on my case,
Nagging or shouting at me for nothing.

My skin is feeling spotty,
I have blackheads on my chin,
My hair is greasy much quicker,
Not showering seems like it's a sin!

I do not know what to do with my hair
To grow it longer or to cut it all off,
I'm scared to wear something different
Incase others will look and laugh.

Ctd…

I am causing some arguments at home right now,
I really do feel bad,
I do not like upsetting people at all,
Or making others feel mad.

I cannot help being in this phase,
For pre-teens it is normal,
Just please know that I will settle down one day
Fingers crossed, not be so hormonal!

Pre - teens workbook.

Is there a special person in your life, that you would talk to if you had a problem? If so who are they and why are they special?

Name three things that make you angry quickly?

1)

2)

3)

Name three things that make you feel better when you are annoyed or irritated?

1)

2)

3)

What would you do if you noticed that your friend was in a bad mood to help them?

NEW SCHOOL

Today I have started a new school,
I am shaking in my shoes,
What if I don't make any friends,
Or know what on earth to do.

I am afraid of not knowing my way around,
Being late for all my lessons,
Then when I finally find the right class,
I have missed half of the session.

What if the teacher tells me off,
Because I do not know how to do my work,
Then everyone laughs and points at me,
They think I am the worlds greatest birk.

At lunch I may have to sit alone,
Cos I do not know anyone there,
When I try to sit down next to someone I am told
"This is someone elses chair".

When it is time for P.E,
No one choses me to be part of their team,
I am stood their last on my own,
I just want to shout and scream.

Ctd…

Everyone gives me funny looks,
They do not know my name,
They ask me why I have come to their school,
I find it difficult to explain.

I have found someone who is nice to me,
They have told me I can sit with them.
I hope I see them tomorrow
Praying they say the same thing again.

New school workbook.

Have you ever had to change schools? If so how did you feel about it?

How did you feel on your very first day at school?

Name your three favourite subjects at school?

1)

2)

3)

What is the name of your best friend/s?

What do you like about them?

NAME CALLING

Why do you always pick on everyone,
You say the most horrible things.
Just cos someone wears glasses,
Or has an unusual name.

You call him skint and a looser,
Just because he doesn't have the latest trainers,
Saying racist names,
Thinking it is ok,
Hurting people's feelings.

Picking on someone just for fun,
Because they are quiet and shy,
Saying nasty things all the time,
Until you make them cry.

Shouting "you're a skeleton",
Just because she is tall and slim,
Calling him names so offensive,
Just cos he has darker skin.

When our friend has a disability,
You think it is ok to laugh,
So cruel, unkind and senseless,
You think you are full of sass!

Ctd…

No-one really likes you,
Your are so mean to their friends,
You think lots of people think you cool,
They just don't want to be on recieveing end.

I think one day you will have no friends,
If you continue to be hurtful,
I hope you grow up to be kind and caring,
To break this vicious circle..

Name calling workbook

Do you think people who are different from you make the world interesting?

Why?

Name three foods you have tried that come from a different country?
1)

2)

3)

Name 2 countries you would like to visit and taste the food?

1)

2)

ADOPTED

Ever since I was a little baby
My parents could not take care of me,
They had far too many problems,
A way out of they could not see.

My Mum she gave birth to me,
She held me then I was taken away,
I wonder if she felt sad,
That with her I could not stay.

It doesn't mean they did not love me,
Or want the best for me,
Infact they wanted me safe and well
With a brand-new family.

I know that they must think of me
Wonder how I am,
If I am tall or short, the colour of my hair,
If I look like my Dad or Mam.

I have been in care for quite a while,
Different families I have been homed in,
I've had to change schools and move around
To find a family I can stay with.

Ctd…

They have not always been nice experiences,
Not everyone is kind,
I didn't always like where I was
Sometimes sad from always moving around.

I have finally been adopted
With other kids altogether we are three,
I cannot tell you how happy I feel,
That someone finally wants me.

Adopted workbook.

How many people live in your house?

Do you share your bedroom? If so who with?

What are your favourite things in your house?

Can you think of some places you would love to visit with your family? List them below.

GRIEF

I know there is some sad news today,
I am trying to be strong,
My Mum will not stop crying,
I know something is very wrong.

My heart is in my tummy,
I do not know what to say,
Sweetheart it's your Daddy,
He has died and flown away!

God wanted him in heaven,
There is a lot for him to do up there,
He is now your very own Angel,
Of you he will take good care.

But what about all of the plans that we made,
He will not see me growing up,
How am I supposed to live without my Dad,
I will miss him so much.

Your daddy wants you to be happy,
To live a wonderful inspiring life,
To try so very hard at school,
Always be strong, brave and kind.

Ctd...

He loves you so very much,
In your heart he will always stay,
Whenever you want to talk to him whisper,
He will hear every word you say.

Mummy promises to love you twice as much,
To always be there for you,
Whenever you are looking up at the stars,
Know that he is looking at you too.

Daddy will be by your side,
Always keep you safe,
Just before you fall asleep at night,
He will gently kiss your face.

Grief workbook.

Is there anyone who you miss? Who?

Can you recall some memories, things you remember that you have done together, either through memory, what people have told you or through photographs? List them below.

Can you remember some special things about them? List them below.

If you could say anything to them now then what would it be?

ONE PARENT

I have never met my Dad,
I do not know who he is,
My Mum says he has never bothered with me,
That's just the way it is.

I wonder why he dosen't want to see me,
I have done nothing to him at all.
My friends are going to their Dad's tonight,
I don't even have a Dad to call.

He never gave us money,
Or asked if there was anything he could do,
He doesn't even know what I look like now,
Or where I go to school.

I suppose I know no different,
My Mum loves me very much,
She works so hard for both of us,
Gave me everything I have got.

Mum wants to give me the best chance in life,
To not miss out on anything.
She wants us to have a peaceful homelife,
Be grateful for everthing.

Ctd…

Even though I only have one parent,
It sometimes makes me feel sad,
Then I remember all my family members,
This makes me feel glad.

I have aunties, uncles and cousins,
We all love each other very much,
We have the best times at Nanny's and Granda's,
Especially when they make us lunch.

I may only have one parent,
But I still feel lucky and glad,
That I have such a wonderful life,
We are not doing too bad!

One parent workbook.

Do you have one parent or two?

Have you ever been on holiday, where to?

What is your favourite game/toys to play with at home?

Do you like a cuddle before you sleep? Who gives it to you?

If you wake up at night, who looks after you?

ARGUING

Here they go again oh no,
Shouting at each other,
Why is it always when I am trying to fall asleep,
They argue louder and louder.

Do they even like one another,
Cos shouting is all I hear,
I use my pillow to block the sound,
But it does not disappear.

I start to feel terrified inside,
I hate it when they fight,
My heart beat is going faster in my chest,
I jump up with the fright.

I don't know what to do right now,
Sleeping is out of the question,
Do I go downstairs and tell them to be quiet,
Or wait for it to lesson?

Slamming doors, bangs and shouts,
I really do not like this at all,
It is always the same most nights,
I wish they would just stop it all.

Ctd...

When I am supposed to be learning at school,
I cannot take anything in,
The teacher tells me, "You can do better that this"
But I cannot seem to win.

When I try to concentrate
My eyes are stinging with tiredness,
I feel my head nodding off,
How on earth can I fix this?

I hope my parents figure it out,
Stop shouting at each other,
So I can fall asleep at night,
Do my work and succeed much better!

Arguing workbook

What makes you feel scared?

Is there anything that you can do to make yourself feel better at the time? If so what?

Do you know that it is ok for you to feel good inside even when something feels scary. I will share with you a little breathing exercise that will keep you calm, by slowing down your heart rate.
If you take short breaths into your nose then blowing out of your mouth like you are letting all of the air out of a balloon. If you keep on doing this it will help.

Why don't you try it?

You can always visulaise yourself doing something out of this world, like scoring a goal for your favourite football team, or meeting your favourite film star. You can day dream and go into your own little magic world, which will with practice help you to feel better and take the attention off the things that are scaring you. Especially when you are in bed. You will fall asleep with positive things in your mind.

BE KIND

You never know what someone is going through
Sometimes life can be so tough,
No one is exempt from problems
Loss, grief, sadness and lots of other stuff.

Some people can feel worried
Scared or maybe in a panic,
When their world is turned upside down
Everything seems so tragic.

Finding life is hard to navigate-
Through all the stress and fear,
Worried for their loved ones;
Feeling that no one is really here.

So always choose to be nice
You never know what they are passing through,
If you notice they are not themselves,
Maybe you are someone they can talk to.

Perhaps they don't want to talk
But just need a friend close by,
To support them and offer a shoulder
When they need to break down and cry.

Ctd…

We all have worries sometimes;
Life can feel like a challenge and a chore,
But nothing lasts forever,
You will feel better once more.

Offer a smile and a friendly hug
Let them know that you care,
When some one has a problem
They always feel better when it is shared.

Be kind workbook

Have you ever felt worried and not known what to do?

What happened?

Name three things you would do to help yourself, if you had a problem.

1)

2)

3)

What would you do to help someone who was passing through a difficult time?

KARMA

I'm told what goes around comes around,
I really want to know if it is true.
That what you put out into the world,
Comes all the way back to you.

We are all made of energy and information,
Right down to every last cell.
We have to be careful how we treat others,
Because we will be treated the same as well.

If we chose to be mean and horrible
Without feeling sorry for our actions,
All we are doing Is opening ourselves up,
To receive the same reactions.

We should try to be kind and helpful;
Always do good deeds.
We never know we might find someone to lean on,
In our time of need.

Karma really is a lesson,
To be the best that we can be
Giving out what we want back,
Helping us decide who we want to be.

Ctd…

Whatever you chose to focus on
Will come right back to you,
So you may as well think of the wonderful things,
The potential surrounding you too.

Violence and cruelty have no place in my life,
Neither lies nor deceit,
I want to manifest the exact opposite of these,
To make my life so sweet.

If I really do have a choice,
Then I want to decide for the best,
To fill myself with love and kindness,
Positive riches and all of the rest.

I like the idea that what I give out,
Will come right back to me,
From now on I will think of the positive things
For my family, friends and me.

Karma workbook

Make a wish list of all of the things you would love to manifest into your life. They can be absoloutley anthing!

Believe that they will come true and they may just!

PLEASE DO NOT WIND ME UP

Please do not wind me up,
Just because you know I will react.
I do not know how to regulate myself,
Will always snap right back.

It is unfair that you provoke me
Then sit back and laugh at me,
When I lose my temper and shout so loud,
Even though I don't want this to be me.

My brain works a little bit differently from yours
I act first then I think after,
Sometimes I cannot think at all
As panic mode just takes over.

If you tell me I have done something you do not like;
My reaction is to lash out,
I don't know how to stop myself,
I have to get all my dissapointment out.

If you interrupt me when I am talking,
This really makes me mad,
I want you to find me interesting
When you don't it makes me sad.

Ctd…

When something really bothers me,
The first thing I do is curse and swear,
Please know that I do not mean these things,
They just come out from thin air.

Just because my reactions are different from yours,
It does not mean that I am not kind and loving,
I really do not want to hurt anyone,
I just need understanding when I am struggling.

Please do not wind me up workbook

Name five things that really wind you up.

1) bullies, who bully me daily

2) Emily, ex-friend (bullies me too)

3) Sophie (second youngest sister)

4) everything

5) everyone

If someone was winding you up on purpose is there anything that you could try and do to stop you from reacting? Think of five things.

1)

2)

3)

4)

5)

MOTHER EARTH

Our world is beautiful and magical,
Let me tell you why,
We live on a big ball of water,
Floating above us is the beautiful sky.

We have an abundance of trees and leaves
That give us oxygen to breathe;
Millions of birds, butterflies, insects, animals,
Lots and lots of human beings.

Mountains, rivers, oceans,
Lakes, jungles, banana plants so high.
Pyramids, Temples the Sahara desert,
Sand dunes that go on for miles.

The sun rises every morning,
To give us life on earth,
The rain nourishes our soil,
Together they cause birth.

Cos if you put a little seed in the soil
Then a flower or potato will grow,
The largest melon you have ever seen
Or grape vines with millions of rows.

Ctd…

Mother Earth fills us with positive energy
Grounding us in nature,
For if you swim in the big blue sea
Then you feel her love and nurture.

The sun is super magnetic
Full of positive vibes,
The moon keeps our earth from tumbling,
Even controls our tides.

The sky is so wondorous
All the different colours it brings,
Massive vast expansiveness
Beyond it can't be seen.

All the planets and their sun's
Leave us curious to know,
How do we move around the sun everday
How does the sky make snow?

The stars so bright bring magic,
We can make wishes and know they will be heard,
I am sure when the stars look down at us
They see us as just the same.

Shining delightful light beams
With lots of colours held within,
If we can take a minute to appreciate,
We can feel the nature in us once again.

Ctd..

We can use all the splendor around us
To inspire us ever day,
Like the birds with their satellite navigation,
We have to use an aeroplane.

How do they know where to go?
Some fly three thousand miles there and back,
Or the salmon that swim through the rivers
Or the ducks that like to quack.

They know where to come back to,
When it is time for their return,
It is like the little robins arrive in your garden
At the same time every year.

We come from and return back to nature
Life is a beautiful magnificent cycle,
We must make the best of our mother earth,
Always do our best to recycle.

Please try and find a few minutes
To connect to nature in any kind of way,
Even taking a few deep conscious breaths,
To fill you up and help you through your day.

Mother Earth Workbook.

Name five things you love about Mother Nature?

1)

2)

3)

4)

5)

Why do you think our earth is special?

Name some things we can do to protect our earth?

DIFFERENT COUNTRY

We have had to change countries,
Leave everyone behind,
My Mum got a job somewhere else
I wasn't even asked if I mind!

Mum said she will be paid a lot more,
She works as a Midwife and Nurse,
She said she can help lots of people back home;
As she will have a lot more money in her purse!

I will really miss my country,
My friends and family too,
I will miss the warm sunshine,
Just everything we do.

We play every day in the sea
Snorkeling and having fun
We pick juicy mango's off the trees
Then share them with everyone.

In the evening we are all out in the street
Each and every family,
Taking turns at cooking the food
It gets shared out equally.

Ctd…

There is always music playing,
How we love to sing and dance,
It doesn't matter what your age is
Everyone has a chance.

I do not know why we need more money,
Or why we have to leave,
Mum says it's for a better life
For our whole community.

So off we go to England,
I am in a new school now,
I cannot speak the language
Making friends is very hard.

People try to talk to me
But I cannot understand a word,
Though everyone seems to be nice and kind,
When I speak I go unheard!

Some children do smile at me,
Sometimes teachers take my hand
I join in with some games
Like playing in the sand.

I do miss home so very much
Our culture and traditions
But I guess I have to find a way
To fall in love with Great Britain.

Different Country Workbook

Have you ever had to change countries? Or do you know someone who has?

How do you think the little person feels having to leave friends, family, cultures and traditions behind?

What do you think the challenges would be when you go to a new school and cannot understand or speak the language?

What are the favourite things about your culture and traditions? List them below.

EVERYONE IS GOOD AT SOMETHING

If you haven't figured out what you are good at,
Then know that there is plenty of time.
Everyone is good at something
You will get to know in time.

Some people are good at Maths or English
Cooking or P.E,
Some people are good at caring for others,
Or climbing high up the trees.

There are some fantastic footballers,
Swimmers and athletes,
Singers, dancers, readers,
Fashion designers, hairstylists.

Maybe you are good at painting nails,
Doing lashes or taking care of skin,
Maybe good at doing makeup,
Acting, or working out in the gym.

Perhaps you will be good at cleaning,
Or playing a musical instrument,
Getting along with people,
Netball, maybe even ski-ing.

Ctd...

It can take a long time
To really get to know,
What you are good at,
Or which path you want to follow,

You may change your mind a million times
It is your choice what you try,
You can be anything you want to,
As long as you feel the positive vibes.

One thing that will definetly help you
Is how you feel inside,
If you find things that you love to do
It will most certainly make you smile.

Everyone is good at something workbook

Do you know what you enjoy to do? If so write them below. (you can enjoy something without having to be really good at it)!

Is there something you haven't tried yet but would love to give it a go? Write them below.

Will you start to notice the feelings inside your body, like when something feels wonderful or something feels uncomfortable? If you know any already list them here;

WONDERFUL FEELINGSUNCOMFORTABLE FEELINGS

If you or anyone you know have been affected by any of the topics or issues raised in this book then please seek advice. Below are some charities that you can call for help. For medical or mental health concerns please contact your G.P or doctors office for advice.

Childline ; 0800 1111

Mind; 0300 1233393

National bullying helpline; 0845 2255787

Step change debt charity; 0800 138 1111

Stop Hate; 0300 123 2220

National bereavement service; 0800 0246 121

Child bereavement UK; 0800 028 8840

Disability rights UK; 0330 945 0400

Refugee Action; 07917 093 159

PAGES FOR YOUR NOTES.

Printed in Great Britain
by Amazon